A Young Citizen's Guide To:

The Electoral System

John Norris

HODDER
Wayland

an imprint of Hodder Children's Books

A Young Citizen's Guide series

Parliament
Local Government
The Electoral System
Central Government
The Criminal Justice System
Voluntary Groups
The Media in Politics
The European Union
Money
Political Parties

Published in Great Britain in 2002 by Hodder Wayland,
an imprint of Hodder Children's Books

Editor: Patience Coster
Series editor: Alex Woolf
Series design: Simon Borrough
Picture research: Glass Onion Pictures
Consultant: Dr Stephen Coleman

British Library Cataloguing in Publication Data
Norris, John
A young citizen's guide to the electoral system
1. Politics, Practical - Great Britain - Juvenile literature
2. Great Britain - Politics and government - 1997 - -
Juvenile literature
I. Title
324.6'3'0941

ISBN 0 7502 3776 7

Printed and bound in Hong
Kong by Wing King Tong

Hodder Children's Books,
a division of Hodder Headline
Limited, 338 Euston Road,
London NW1 3BH

Picture acknowledgements:
the publisher would like to thank
the following for permission to use
their pictures: Mary Evans Picture
Library 9, 10; Impact 4 (Petteri
Kokkonen), 22 (Piers Cavendish),
25 (Stefan Boners/Ipon);
Popperfoto 11, 23;
Popperfoto/Reuter 7, 8, 14 and
contents page, 15, 16, 19, 20,
21 and title page; Press
Association/Topham 5, 6, 13, 26,
27, 28; Topham Picturepoint 18.

Cover: people outside a polling
station (Topham); counting the
votes during Euro elections in
Gwent (Eye Ubiquitous/Paul
Stuart); general election, June
2001 (Impact/Z Lightfoot).

Contents

The electoral system is the means by which we elect our representatives in a democracy. The word democracy comes from the Greek words 'demos', meaning 'the people', and 'Kratos', meaning 'to rule'. The United Kingdom is a representative democracy, which means that the people elect politicians (Members of Parliament or MPs, Euro-MPs, local councillors, and so on) who represent their views in a variety of places (Parliament, the European Parliament, local town halls etc.).

Leaving a polling station after casting a vote in a local government election.

In the United Kingdom, people over the age of eighteen can vote in a range of elections, including:

- general elections – by which MPs are elected to Parliament in Westminster;
- European elections – by which MEPs are elected to the European Parliament in Strasbourg;
- local government elections – by which councillors are elected to local councils;
- regional elections – by which representatives are elected (by people living in Scotland or Wales) to the Scottish Parliament and Welsh Assembly.

Elected representatives

In Ancient Greece, all adult males would meet together to discuss their ideas and pass new laws. (Females and slaves, however, were not allowed to vote.) This system was called a direct democracy. Such a system would be impractical in today's crowded world, so we elect others to do the job for us! These people are known as elected representatives.

A political party is a body of people who share similar ideas about the kind of society they wish to live in. Most candidates who stand in elections belong to one political party or another. Candidates who do not belong to political parties are called Independents.

Elections are a vital part of our way of life. Without them, we would not have the opportunity to influence government on things that matter to us. Look at the list of important questions that have been discussed in recent years:

- Should fox-hunting be banned?
- Should the United Kingdom replace the pound with the European Single Currency?
- Should we spend more money on the National Health Service and schools? Are we prepared to pay extra taxes to fund improved health and education services?
- Should genetically modified crops be allowed?
- Should young people be prevented from going out on the streets late at night?

These issues affect all our lives – what are your views on them?

Trying to influence potential voters? This Liberal Democrat is standing in a local bye-election. Candidates like to support popular causes, such as family issues.

'I decided to enter local government because I am profoundly committed to the idea that people need to participate in the mechanisms of government if we are going to make society a better place.... Democracy is a fragile flower and it needs all the nurture it can get!' Peter Downes, councillor for the Liberal Democrats, Brampton Ward, Huntingdon, Cambridgeshire.

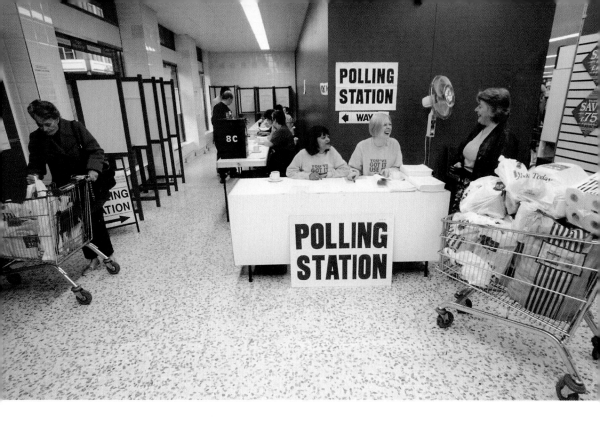

To vote, or not to vote?

To vote, or not to vote? Some people believe that all the citizens of a country have a responsibility to vote in an election. Others believe it is a matter of individual choice. The percentage of registered voters who actually do vote is known as the 'turnout'. In the United Kingdom the turnout is quite high – around 70-75 per cent. However, in the 2001 UK general election the turnout fell to 59.2 per cent, the lowest recorded this century. In the constituency of Liverpool Riverside, only 34.1 per cent of the electorate voted.

There are various reasons why some people do not vote. One reason is that the electoral register (the list of those entitled to vote) is always slightly out of date, and some of the people on it may have died. Others may have moved out of the area. Another reason is that some people feel that their views are not represented by the major parties; some sections of the community are 'apathetic', in other words they cannot be bothered to cast their votes.

Shoppers casting their votes at a mobile polling station in a supermarket in 1997.

A mobile polling station in the Australian outback (right). In Australia, the turnout is almost 100 per cent. This is because voting is compulsory there. Would you like to see such a system in the UK?

In 2001, it was suggested that, as Labour was strongly tipped to win the general election, this discouraged people from voting in 'safe' Labour seats. There is some evidence to support this, as the turnout in 'marginal' (closely contested) seats was, on average, higher than in safe seats.

A high turnout is considered to be a sign of a healthy democracy. In recent years various methods have been suggested to encourage more people to vote. These include:

- making it easy to register as a voter;
- using mobile polling stations (the centres at which voting takes place), which could be located at places of work, colleges, hospitals, supermarkets, railway stations and on high streets;
- holding elections at weekends;
- voting over a period of two or three days, rather than on one day;
- voting on the internet.

Party manifestos
Political parties present their ideas in documents called manifestos. Here are some examples of the main parties' manifesto headlines for the UK general election of 2001.

A REAL CHANCE FOR A REAL CHANGE
(the Liberal Party)

AMBITIOUS FOR BRITAIN
(the Labour Party)

TIME FOR COMMON SENSE
(the Conservative Party)

The political parties try to create manifesto titles that are 'catchy' and convince potential voters of their reliability and competence. Often these headline slogans are repeated for emphasis in the parties' general election campaign, for example on posters and in television advertising.

It is worth considering at this point how easy it is for us to take our right to vote for granted. The United Nations estimate that more than half the world's people live in societies where they do not have the right to vote, and are therefore unable to change their governments by peaceful means. In recent years, democracy movements have fought for the right to vote in countries such as China and Indonesia. In these countries, the government often controls the political parties (where they are allowed to exist) and the mass media. Under such circumstances, it is very difficult for ordinary citizens to effect political change.

In the United Kingdom, the right to vote for all adults has only existed for just over seventy years. Writing in 1787, the American, James Maddison said: 'the price of liberty is eternal vigilance'. One of the ways to maintain our vigilance (in other words, to keep an eye on our representatives) is to vote for a particular candidate at election time.

The disadvantage of free elections is that you never know who is going to win them.' V M Molotov, Soviet Foreign Minister, 1946.

Democracy comes to South Africa. Black people cast their votes alongside white people for the first time in multiracial elections in 1994.

The History of the Electoral System

In 1815, the United Kingdom was a largely agricultural nation. Most of its population of nineteen million lived in the countryside. The political system was dominated by the aristocracy, and less than 5 per cent of the people could vote. A requirement for voting was that a man (women were not allowed to vote) should own a substantial amount of property.

The more populated areas of the country were known as boroughs. In what became known as the 'rotten boroughs', Members of Parliament were appointed without any votes being cast. In such cases, the MPs were simply chosen by the most powerful and wealthy landowner in the area. On the occasions when voting took place, there was no secret ballot. Local landowners often controlled the results of elections and pressured people to vote for a particular candidate – sometimes people voted in public by raising their hands! Corruption of this kind, including the bribing of voters, was widespread in the rotten boroughs, and some parliamentary seats were openly bought and sold.

Voting in a rotten borough in 1758.

New demands By the beginning of the nineteenth century, people had begun to flock from the countryside to work in the new factories in towns and cities. Various groups were formed – workers, shopkeepers and the owners of industries – and they began to demand the right to elect their MPs.

This 'industrial revolution' led to demands for improved housing, sanitation and working conditions. The pressure on governments to allow more people to vote grew steadily.

Voting reforms In 1832, Parliament passed the Great Reform Act. This Act only increased the size of the electorate by 5 per cent, but it was a major first step. The Prime Minister, Earl Grey, also began to create constituencies by population. This move benefited city-dwellers, as the populous centres of new industry gained more seats in the House of Commons.

The Reform League was a group of people who argued for changes to the political system and campaigned for the right of all workers to vote. In response to pressure from this group, Parliament passed a further Act in 1867 which gave the vote to homeowners and, somewhat bizarrely, to ten rent payers in every town! So now two million people had the vote. The Ballot Act of 1872 made all voting secret, thus reducing the dangers of bribery and intimidation in voting procedures. In 1884, a further 12 per cent of men were given the vote. Towards the end of the nineteenth century, political parties became increasingly large organizations, as they sought to win the votes of the new electorate.

Members of the Reform League address a political rally in Birmingham to press the case for the Great Reform Bill of 1832.

Female emancipation Throughout the nineteenth century, some women argued for their right to vote. These women were, in the main, from the upper classes, and therefore had the time and the freedom to lobby for their cause. They were known as suffragettes, a name derived from the word 'suffrage', meaning the right to vote. During the First World War, the campaign for female emancipation (votes for women) became particularly influential. As most able-bodied men were needed to fight for their country, there was a labour shortage between 1914 and 1918. During these years, many women learned new skills and worked in industries that were normally the preserve of men. If they were capable of this, then why should they not have the right to vote?

Eventually, in 1918, all women over the age of thirty and all men over the age of twenty-one were given the right to vote. The first female MP to enter the House of Commons was Nancy, Viscountess Astor, in 1919. And in 1928 the inequality between the voting ages of men and women was removed when all women over the age of twenty-one gained the vote. In 1969, the voting age was reduced from twenty-one to eighteen. At the start of the twenty-first century, some people argue that because teenagers begin to enjoy many adult rights at the age of sixteen, the voting age should be reduced further. This may well be a debate for the future.

Date	% of adults with the vote
1832	5
1867	13
1884	25
1918	75
1928	99
1969	99

You will notice that the figures for 1928 and 1969 are identical. This is because the definition of 'adult' changed from aged twenty-one to aged eighteen. The 1 per cent who cannot vote includes people not on the electoral register.

11

How Does the Electoral System Work?

In order to be able to vote in an election in the United Kingdom, your name must be entered on the electoral register of the constituency (the geographical area that is represented by a Member of Parliament) in which you live. The electoral register is drawn up every year by an official known as the local registration officer. To get your name on the register you must:

- be eighteen years of age;
- be a British subject;
- have a fixed address.

'The best thing about the campaign was that it stirred up young people, which is very important.... People who had been totally disenchanted with party politics got interested.'
Independent MP Martin Bell, talking about his election campaign in 1997.

There are some people who are not allowed to vote. They include peers, aliens (not of the ET variety, but people who do not have citizenship!), people judged insane, people in prison for certain offences and people who have been convicted of corrupt election practices. Citizens of Eire (southern Ireland) who have lived in the UK for three months continuously are allowed to vote.

Why do people vote? Some people vote because they know how hard our ancestors fought for the right to do so. Others vote because they wish to express their views on the important question of who will form the next government. In practice, all voters must vote for individual candidates, but generally speaking people tend to vote for the political party that their candidate represents.

The candidates Any British citizen over the age of twenty-one may stand for election, apart from members of the police and armed forces, certain civil servants, judges, and Anglican and Roman Catholic clergy.

Constituency boundaries There are 659 UK parliamentary constituencies. The average population of a constituency is 65,000. It is the job of an organization called the Boundary Commission to make sure that constituencies are more or less the same size. This is because it would not be fair if one MP represented 20,000 voters, while another represented 100,000, as the number of votes required to win a seat in Parliament could vary drastically. The Boundary Commission compiles a report every ten to fifteen years and recommends any changes needed to try and maintain a fair system. In recent years, the south-east of England has gained extra seats, while city areas have lost seats. This shift reflects population changes, as some people have moved out of the cities into the suburbs and adjacent countryside.

While the police help to ensure our free elections they are, ironically, not allowed to stand as candidates themselves.

General elections

In the UK, a general election must be held at least once every five years. The date of the election is not fixed by law but decided by the Prime Minister, who traditionally consults the monarch (this is because the monarch still holds the constitutional post of Head of State). Some countries have 'fixed term' elections, where everyone knows the date of the election in advance. Some people would prefer to have fixed term elections in the UK; these would make it more difficult for a Prime Minister to call a general election at the best time for the government, for example, when the economy was doing well.

'...people say elections are tough and gruelling and, up to a point, they are, but they are also a lot of fun... '
Prime Minister John Major, during the 1997 campaign.

The run-up to a general election is called the campaign. The political parties campaign – present their manifestos to the electorate – both locally and nationally. Locally, teams of helpers called 'canvassers' distribute leaflets and posters, talk to voters on their doorstep and try to ensure that their candidate wins the constituency. Nationally, the political parties produce 'party election broadcasts' that are transmitted on television and radio – these broadcasts represent the policies of the party concerned in the best possible light. Radio, newspapers and the internet carry advertisements. The leaders of the various political parties travel across the country, paying special attention to 'marginal' seats (those which are expected to have a very close result). Despite all this effort, most people will have decided which candidate to vote for before the campaign begins. However, election campaigning may persuade 'floating voters' (people who have not made up their minds) to vote for a particular party.

Can we count on your vote? A canvasser on a voter's doorstep.

Predicting the winner

Throughout the campaign, opinion polls are carried out to discover how people intend to vote. The political parties often carry out their own opinion polls, but newspapers, television and radio often use the findings of national organizations such as MORI and NOP. An opinion poll is a survey of the views of between one and two thousand voters chosen randomly from the electorate. Occasionally you may see interviewers asking members of the public questions for opinion polls in town centres during an election campaign.

Opinion polls have a good record of predicting who will win an election. They claim to be accurate to within 3 per cent. However, in 1992, the polls overestimated the Labour Party's share of the vote by 4 per cent and underestimated the Conservative Party's by the same amount. Despite predicting a Labour victory of 9 per cent, the Conservatives won by 7.6 per cent!

Opinion polls – why they sometimes get it wrong

A late swing Undecided voters might make their minds up only on the day of the election.

Turnout Perhaps more Conservative voters turned out to vote in 1992 and some Labour voters stayed at home.

Non-registration Some people interviewed by the pollsters may not have registered to vote.

'The truth factor' There is evidence to suggest that some people may tell the interviewers they are going to vote for one party, but on election day actually vote for the opposing party.

Preparing to do battle during a televised debate. John Prescott (left) for Labour and Michael Heseltine (right) for the Conservatives during the 1997 general election campaign.

Voting

On election day, members of the public who wish to vote go to polling stations, which are situated in local schools, sports centres etc. throughout the constituency. Each potential voter will have previously registered his or her right to vote and received a polling card. Even if voters forget or lose their polling cards, they can still vote by having their name and address checked by the officials running the polling station.

Once the voter's name has been checked, he or she is given a ballot paper, which contains the names of the candidates and their political parties. Voting is very simple – voters write an X in the box next to their chosen candidate and then place their ballot paper in the ballot box.

Once the polling stations close (usually at 10.00 pm), all the ballot boxes are sealed and taken to a central counting place (such as a town hall) where teams of election officials undertake the 'count'. In UK general and local elections, counting is very straightforward. This is because the 'first-past-the-post' system is used. This means that one candidate has to win a 'simple majority' of the votes cast, that is, more votes than any other candidate.

Election results

On election night, the results are announced constituency by constituency by returning officers. The party that receives the most votes in any constituency wins the seat, and its representative becomes the Member of Parliament. To win the election and form a government, a political party needs to win more seats than all of its rivals put

'We do not want a personal and abusive campaign. Let's talk about what we can do for the country.'
Labour leader Tony Blair, during the 1997 general election campaign.

Counting the votes. On election night, many constituencies compete with one another to be the first to declare their results.

together. While this is the usual situation, it is by no means always the case. Sometimes the election results in a 'hung Parliament' where no single party has an absolute majority. In this situation, it is likely that the leader of the largest party would begin discussions with the leader of one of the smaller parties to see whether, together, they could form the next government. When two or more parties form a government, it is known as a 'coalition'.

BALLOT PAPER **Place an X against the candidate of your choice**

Diane Jones
(the Labour Party)

Peter Biggs
(the Conservative Party)

Andrew Carter
(the Liberal-Democrat Party)

Susan Parker
(the Green Party)

Thomas Mann
(the Independent Party)

After the general election, the leader of the winning party (who is also an MP) becomes Prime Minister. In some countries, like France and the USA, separate elections are held for the President. This is because these countries are republics, with a President who is Head of State and elected directly by the people. Britain has an unelected monarch (the Queen) as Head of State. However, while the Queen has the right to express her opinions on government matters, the Prime Minister presides over the formation of the government and heads his or her party in the House of Commons. That way he or she can be reasonably confident of pushing party policies through Parliament.

A ballot paper from a UK general election illustrates the simplicity of the British system.

Local government elections

Councillors are elected using the first-past-the-post system, and serve terms of four years. The areas they represent are called wards. In some areas, notably cities, one-third of the council is elected

17

every four years. The turnout in British local elections is low, often less than 40 per cent. In Luxembourg and Italy it is more than 80 per cent.

In recent years, local government has tried to increase people's interest in its activities by:

- allowing public questions at council meetings;
- creating 'citizens' juries' of between twelve and twenty people to look at particular local issues;
- creating neighbourhood committees;
- encouraging tenants' and residents' groups;
- creating user group forums, made up of members of the public who use a particular service, e.g. transport;
- using the internet to convey information and allow people to respond.

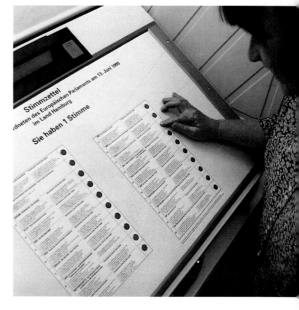

An example of electronic voting in Hamburg, Germany, during the 1999 European elections.

European and regional elections

Members of the European Parliament (MEPs) are elected for four-year terms. The size of their populations determines the number of representatives to which each country is entitled. Thus the UK has eighty-seven MEPs, Germany ninety-nine, but tiny Luxembourg only six. In Scotland, 129 MSPs (members of the Scottish Parliament) are elected. In Wales, sixty members are elected to the 'Senedd', or Welsh Assembly, in Cardiff. And in Northern Ireland there are 108 members elected from eighteen constituencies.

Electing a mayor
On 4 May 2000, Londoners went to the polls for the first time in more than fifteen years to elect a mayor for London. After an exciting campaign, Ken Livingstone was elected using the Supplementary Vote System, a form of proportional representation (see chapter 4).

How Fair is the Electoral System?

The first-past-the-post electoral system used in Britain is sometimes referred to as a 'simple majority' or 'winner takes all' system. The reason for this is quite straightforward: in order to win a constituency, a candidate has to get more votes than anyone else. A candidate is not required to win an absolute majority (in other words, more than 50 per cent of the total votes cast).

In 1999, a new Scottish Parliament was created. Many voters, especially those not living in England, like the idea of shifting a certain amount of power away from central government in London.

Look at the following election results using the first-past-the-post system:

Basingstoke constituency – general election result, June 2001

A Hunter	**Conservative Party**	20,490 votes	42.7%
J Hartley	**Labour Party**	19,610 votes	40.9%
S Sollitt	**Liberal Democrat Party**	6,693 votes	14.0%
K Graham	**UK Independence Party**	1,202 votes	2.5%

Look at the table of national results below and see whether you can spot any injustices in the system.

General election results, June 1983	Party	Seats	%	% Vote
Conservative government	Con	397	61.1	42.4
Majority = 143	Lab	209	32.2	27.6
Turnout = 72.7%	Alliance	23	3.5	25.4
	Others	21	3.2	4.6

In 1983, the Liberal-SDP Alliance won over a quarter of the popular vote, but only gained twenty-three seats. The Liberal Democrat Party regularly wins around 20 per cent of the votes cast nationally, yet gains only a small number of seats – certainly nothing like the number it would win if the system was a proportional one. The reason for this is that, despite the fact that the Liberals win the second-highest number of votes in many seats, there are 'no prizes for coming second' in the first-past-the-post system.

The winning party that forms the government very rarely wins more than 50 per cent of the total votes cast nationally. In that sense, therefore, all our governments represent only a minority of voters. Also, the current system rewards those parties that can concentrate their votes in certain regions. From the table, it is clear that 'others' – including the Scottish and Welsh parties and the Ulster Unionists in Northern Ireland – do quite well in relation to the size of their vote.

ELECTIONS

REGIONALES

A French ballot box. Some regions of France use a system of proportional representation.

Many European countries, such as France, Germany and Italy, use systems which try to ensure that a majority of voters have the final say in who forms a government and that minority voices do not go unrepresented. Many of these systems are based on proportional representation (PR).

With proportional representation, the percentage of seats a party wins in an election is in proportion to the percentage of votes that party receives. There are several different types of proportional representation, including the Single Transferable Vote (STV) and the Additional Member System (AMS).

The Single Transferable Vote (STV)

With this system, as many as four MPs may be elected from a single constituency. Voters have the opportunity to rank candidates in order of preference. So while voters place an X against a single candidate's name in the first-past-the-post system, in the STV system voters number their choice of four candidates in order of preference. The STV system is currently used in Eire. With STV, the constituencies are much bigger than they are with the first-past-the-post system. While constituencies in the UK average 65,000, an STV constituency may be as large as 200,000.

' ... it maximises voter choice, giving the elector power to express preference not only between parties but between different candidates of the same party. It achieves a high degree of proportionality.'
From the Jenkins Report, concerning the Single Transferable Vote, October 1998.

Don't throw your votes away! An STV ballot box being emptied during the count in Dublin, Eire, in 1997.

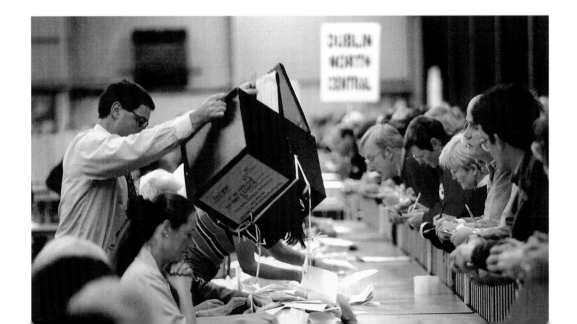

Have a look at the STV ballot paper below. You will notice that not all the political parties have more than one candidate. Indeed, some of the smaller parties may only want one of their candidate's names to appear on the ballot paper so that they can concentrate their votes to their best advantage.

Paddy Ashdown, former leader of the Liberal Democrats, with a young supporter. The Liberal Democrats have long insisted that PR is the fairest way to elect political representatives.

STV ballot paper

Name of Candidate

4	Smith, Alan	**Conservative Party**
5	Green, Susan	**Labour Party**
	Ellison, Steven	**Liberal Party**
6	Lazenby, Cherry	**Conservative Party**
1	Daw, Andrew	**Labour Party**
2	Sainsbury, Peter	**Liberal Party**
3	Hann, Caroline	**Green Party**
	Stanford, Christine	**Referendum Party**

To be elected under the STV system, a candidate must reach what is called the quota. This is a formula that looks horribly complicated:

$$\frac{\text{(number of votes cast)}}{\text{(number of seats +1)}} +1$$

So, for example, if 200,000 votes were cast and four seats were available, then:

$$\frac{\text{(200,000 votes cast)}}{\text{(4 seats available +1)}} +1=40,001 \text{ votes needed}$$

If candidates get past the quota then their surplus votes are redistributed. This is done by firstly working out how many surplus votes they have. Using the above examples, if a candidate received

50,001 votes after the first count, then he or she would have a surplus of 10,000 votes, which are, in effect, 'wasted votes'. In this case, the second choice of all those who voted for this candidate would be counted (all 50,001 votes) and turned into percentages of the candidate's total vote. If, for example, 10,000 second choices have gone to another candidate, then 20 per cent of the surplus votes are allocated; in other words, 20 per cent of 10,000 (2,000 votes).

If, after the surplus votes are redistributed, no candidates reach the quota, then the candidate with the smallest number of votes is eliminated. Then his or her supporters' second choices are distributed to the remaining candidates. This process is repeated until the required number of candidates is elected.

Although STV seems a very complicated system, a computer can be used to help with the technical tasks of vote counting and redistribution. The main point to remember about STV is that it would enable the third party to win more seats. The *Guardian* newspaper has estimated that the Liberal Democrats would have won 115 seats in the 1997 general election had STV been used; with the existing first-past-the-post system they won only forty-six seats.

Another advantage of the STV system is that the voters are allowed to express a preference for the candidate of their choice from the same party. Some people believe that this would result in more female candidates, and perhaps candidates from ethnic minority groups being elected. So, for example, if a Conservative voter wanted to see more female MPs in the House of Commons, he or she could place a 1 next to a female Conservative candidate.

STV allows the voter to choose not only a party, but also a political candidate. Dianne Abbot (below) is currently one of the few black, female MPs in Parliament. Perhaps STV would help to increase the representation of women and ethnic minorities in the House of Commons.

The Additional Member System

In this system, which is used in Germany, voters have two choices. Firstly, they vote for an individual candidate, and secondly, they vote for a political party. Look at the ballot paper below.

When the votes are counted for the individual candidates, the person with the most votes wins – just like the first-past-the-post system. However when the party votes are counted, seats are allocated so that each party gains the number of seats in the German Parliament's upper chamber that is proportional to its share of the vote. In this way smaller parties like the Liberals and the Greens do not lose out!

So why don't we change our voting system in the United Kingdom? Arguments exist for and against electoral reform. Those in favour of our current system tend to emphasize that the first-past-the-post method is simple, straightforward, and produces a clear-cut winner. They point out that it is not really fair to take voters' second and third choices to be equally as important as their first choices. Also, the proportional representation system is likely to result in the election of a coalition government (a government made up of more than one political party). While this might seem sensible, it could make it possible for a small party to have the deciding say on who should form the next government. For example, throughout the post-war period in Germany, the Liberal Party, with

Ballot paper

Mark with a cross the candidate you wish to vote for

Dave Setchell
(Labour Party)   ☐

Duncan Woodall
(Conservative Party)   ☐

Carolyn Price
(Liberal Party)   ☐

Janie Parkin
(Green Party)   ☐

Mark with a cross the party you wish to vote for

Labour Party   ☐

Conservative Party   ☐

Liberal Party   ☐

Green Party   ☐

only 10 per cent of the national vote, has consistently remained in government. In other countries, such as Israel, small nationalist parties have recently held the 'balance of power'. This means that the vote is split so many ways that the largest party in the country cannot form a government without the support of the smaller party(ies).

On the other hand, those in favour of proportional representation continue to emphasize the unfairness of our current system. They point out that it benefits the two largest parties and discriminates against the third party. They also stress that the UK system leads to millions of wasted votes, as the government represents only a minority of voters (usually around 45 per cent).

However, it is by no means certain that any change to our electoral system will take place in the immediate future. One of the ironies of our current system is that electoral change needs the support of at least one of our larger parties, and currently both benefit from the first-past-the-post system.

The German Parliament (below) uses the Additional Member System when electing MPs.

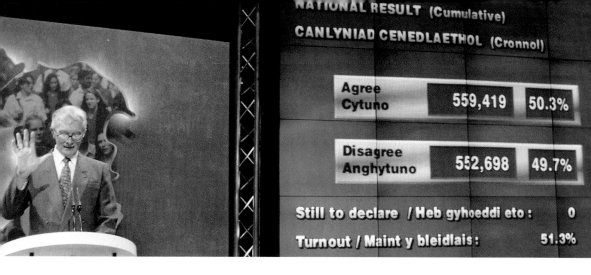

| Agree Cytuno | 559,419 | 50.3% |
| Disagree Anghytuno | 552,698 | 49.7% |

Still to declare / Heb gyhoeddi eto : 0

Turnout / Maint y bleidlais : 51.3%

Referendums So far, we have looked at elections as a means of enabling voters to make a choice about which political party should form a government. The political parties set out their policies in documents called manifestos. The winning party that forms the government then claims a mandate from the people (which means that the voters have given the winning party permission to carry out its policies). But one of the problems with this is that, in a perfect world, we might want to vote for the Liberals because we prefer their policy towards the National Health Service. And we might also want to vote for the Conservatives because we like their education policies, and for Labour because we are attracted to their ideas about law and order.

Of course, we only have one vote, so we have to look at all the parties' policies, and make our overall choice. However, there is a means by which voters can express their preferences on one particular issue, and that is by way of a referendum. In a typical referendum, an issue of public importance is submitted to the direct vote of the electorate, who are asked to express an opinion, usually in the form of a 'yes' or 'no'. In the UK, referendums have been used for deciding on membership of the European Community in 1975, and on Scottish and Welsh

Although it promised to give Welsh people a greater say in their own affairs, the devolution referendum of 1997 (above) was a close-run affair.

> **'Referendums are devices alien to our traditions.'**
> Prime Minister Clement Attlee, 1948.

devolution in 1997. Indeed, all the major political parties are committed to holding a referendum on the issue of the European Single Currency (and a political party, appropriately called the Referendum Party, campaigned on this one issue in the 1997 general election).

The Referendum Party playing with words during its 1997 election campaign.

Ask the people!

In countries such as Switzerland and the United States referendums are held much more frequently than in the UK. Since 1850 there have been nearly 500 referendums in Switzerland. In the USA, many individual states regularly use referendums. For example, the people of California have voted to reduce their taxes and have also reduced the amount of free health-care for illegal immigrants.

Some people would like to see a greater use of referendums in the United Kingdom. They point out that referendums encourage people to take a more active interest in the social, economic and political life of the country. In addition, they give the ordinary voter the right to express their views on issues that are important to them, issues which elected politicians might sometimes prefer to avoid. However, other people believe that politicians are better equipped to take difficult decisions, as they are more familiar with the details and consequences of complicated political issues. In the future it is unlikely that the United Kingdom will have many referendums. However it is possible that there will be one on whether to change our electoral system. You might like to think about how you would vote on this important issue.

> **'Just why does the politician think he is better than me in taking decisions?'**
> From the home page of the Campaign for Direct Democracy, a pressure group in favour of the greater use of referendums in the UK.

Although you cannot vote until you are eighteen, you can still become an informed citizen and participate in the political life of our country. Within your community there will be many pressure groups campaigning for local causes such as education, transport, health, the environment and so on. You could find out more about a concern that interests you and write to local newspapers, or to your MP and local councillors, or contact local radio and TV stations. Nationally there are organizations that campaign on issues they consider to be important. Hansard, in co-operation with the BBC, encourages schools to participate in mock general elections, and these can be great fun.

Your lessons at school will cover the new national curriculum subject of citizenship, and the more knowledgeable and informed you are, the more your fellow students and teachers will sit up and take notice of your views! At home, various members of your family may be prepared to discuss their views on political issues.

Remember, in order to be effective citizens we need to know what is going on in the world around us. No one has all the right answers, but by learning more about our system of politics, we can make sure we ask the right questions!

Happy birthday! A young citizen exercising her right to vote for the first time in 1997.

Getting involved in school life

In most schools, students are allowed to run school councils. The pupils often elect council members themselves. In council meetings the students can raise issues that concern them, such as school facilities for studying, leisure and catering arrangements, and so on. Some schools allow their councils to operate small budgets. Becoming a member of a school council is an excellent start for any student who is interested in politics. It offers students a chance to practise expressing their views, and teaches them to listen to other students' opinions, make difficult decisions and represent one another – almost like being a junior MP!

Activity

Organize your own school general election in ten easy steps.

1 Talk to your teachers beforehand! The more they support your plans and ideas, the smoother the whole process will be! You need to set a time limit (say, one month) for the general election. Week 1 for planning and publicity, week 2 for research, week 3 for campaigning and week 4 for the election and the results.

2 Announce in assembly that the election is taking place. Fix dates and meeting places for those students who would like to be official candidates, or help organize the campaign. Get them to choose one official candidate. Decide how many independent candidates are to be allowed – while one or two might be fun, too many might trivialize your election.

3 Contact local politicians (MPs and councillors) and invite them to take part in a debate in school. Ask local party headquarters for help. Tell local newspapers about the event.

4 In consultation with the candidates, choose your electoral system (you should be an expert by now!). It is quite possible to use two systems at the same time, but expect two sets of results.

5 Encourage your candidates to research the policies of their chosen parties. Use the addresses and web sites at the end of this book.

6 Get candidates to produce manifestos, posters, leaflets, badges etc. Invite them to address school assemblies.

7 Ask the art/design departments to help you make ballot boxes, ballot papers, signposts, information sheets/instructions for election day.

8 Organize the 'hustings' (candidates and their teams to meet together in a classroom/school hall and display their policies, and meet and persuade the voters).

9 Election day. Supervise the voting. Use form/tutor group lists to check off the electorate. Make sure there is no corruption!

10 Count the votes and have the results announced officially to the whole school, if possible by a returning officer. The winning candidate should make an acceptance speech and thank his/her team and the voters.

Glossary

absolute majority the winning of at least 50 per cent of the votes cast

boundary commission an organization that takes account of population changes when setting constituency boundaries

bye-election an election held mid-term, when a seat is vacated

campaign the weeks leading up to an election, during which the political parties compete for votes

canvassers people who help to organize local campaigns, such as delivering leaflets etc.

coalition government a government made up of two or more political parties

constituency the area represented by an MP

democracy a system of government based on free and fair elections

direct democracy a system of elections in which the voters themselves pass laws

electoral register the official list of those who are entitled to vote

electorate the voters

first-past-the-post the system of voting for British general elections, whereby the candidate with the most votes wins

fixed-term elections elections in which the polling dates are set in advance

floating voters voters with no strong allegiance to any political party

franchise those people entitled to vote

hung Parliament a Parliament in which no single party has an absolute majority

Independents candidates standing for election who do not belong to a political party

mandate the consent of the voters given to the party that wins an election

manifesto a document produced at election time containing the policies of a political party

marginal seats constituencies in which candidates have won with very small majorities

media the collective name given to radio, television and the press

MEPs members of the European Parliament

MPs Members of Parliament who sit in the House of Commons

opinion polls samples of the voters' views on their voting intentions and other issues

political parties organizations of like-minded people who try to win elections

polling stations places where people vote

pressure groups organizations that represent their members' interests and try to persuade governments to act on their behalf

proportional representation an electoral system which ensures that the percentage of votes cast equals the percentage of seats won

representative democracy a system of government in which voters elect representatives

returning officer an official who presides over the election in each constituency and announces the results

simple majority the situation that arises when a candidate receives more votes than any other candidate

turnout the percentage of registered voters who actually vote

Resources

To find out more about citizenship itself, try the following web sites:

http://home.clara.net/citizen/home.html
the Centre for Citizenship: this has all kinds of information on British democracy and about whether the UK should become a republic (in other words, have no monarch as Head of State)

http://www.citfou.org.uk/ the Citizenship Foundation: promotes citizenship education, including human rights

http://www.timeforcitizenship.com/
Time for Citizenship: a new site backed by teachers, the police, the NSPCC and the government

To find out more about different electoral systems, try:

http://www.psr.keele.ac.uk/election.htm
Elections and electoral systems by country

If you want to contact your local MP and look at election results constituency by constituency, try:

http://www.psr.keele.ac.uk/area/uk/mps.htm

For an in-depth look at the British general election results of 2001, go to:

http://www.psr.keele.ac.uk/area/uk/ge97.htm

Political parties are always interested to hear the views of young people and most of them have a young persons' section. To look at their manifestos, try:

www.psr.keele.ac.uk/table/man.htm

The major political parties can be contacted at the following sites:

http://www.conservative-party.org.uk/
the Conservative Party

http://www.labour.org.uk/ the Labour Party

http://www.libdems.org.uk/ the Liberal Democrat Party

http://www.greenparty.org.uk/ the Green Party

http://www.snp.org.uk/ the Scottish National Party

http://www.political.org.uk/group/pc.html
Plaid Cymru

http://sinnfein.ie/ Sinn Fein

http://www.uup.org/ Ulster Unionist Party

Visit www.learn.co.uk for more resources.

learn.co.uk
from *The* **Guardian**

Index

Numbers in **bold** refer to illustrations.